Mama's in the Kitchen

By

Barbara Swell

Home

"A LITTLE HOUSE
- BUT IT'S ALL OUR OWN
A PLACE TO LOVE
    A PLACE CALLED HOME "

ISBN: 1-883206-39-1   Order No. NGB-835
Library of Congress Control Number: 2002103200
©2002 by Native Ground Music, Inc.
Asheville, North Carolina

INTRODUCTION

M ama's in the kitchen cooking up a storm. She's making her famous meatloaf and a trendy gelatin parfait that's chilling right now in her electric refrigerator. She'll tell you that, when she was raised up, women stayed home to take care of house and family. But did you ever wonder what life was really like for her growing up? Well, I'll tell you.

During the years between 1900 and 1950, dramatic changes occurred for women as technology arrived on the homefront. Electric ranges replaced wood and coal cookstoves. Clothes washed by hand in large outside cauldrons were now cleaned by gasoline or electric washing machines. There were electric vacuum cleaners, refrigerators, and mixers designed to give busy housewives a break. You'd think these newfangled devices would have saved time, but standards just got tougher. Clothes once washed weekly could now be washed daily. Women were encouraged to keep their homes spotless as they became influenced by product advertising. The time spent by housewives performing housekeeping tasks actually increased as society demanded so much more of them.

 You might assume that the women of this era were an oppressed, miserable, tired, and passive lot. Quite the contrary. The women whose cookbooks I've read were strong-minded, energetic, spicy, warm, and passionate about their lives. They proudly carried their family, community and country on their backs through two world wars, food shortages, a horrendous flu epidemic, and the Great Depression.

Here you'll find the stories of our mothers and grandmothers as they cooked their way through some of the most difficult decades in American history. You'll also get a good glimpse at the expectations placed on women by popular food advertisers. I had every intention of writing a serious book about hard times, but the many vintage advertising cookbooks and handwritten cooking manuscripts I consulted were so very funny by today's standards that I laughed all the way through this project. All of the recipes included are as originally written. Some are great, others will surely knot your stomach. Have fun!

CONTENTS

INDEX OF RECIPES

1900-1919

Up until 1920, cooking was fairly straightforward for the average family. Folks in rural areas grew and preserved their own food. In urban areas, women shopped daily. Meat was roasted in one piece, leftovers were chopped up and eaten in various forms the next day. The dessert you prepared depended on the availability and cost of ingredients. Recipes were handed-down, traded, or clipped from newspapers.

Young women, however, were wanting to spend less time in the kitchen and more time out of the home working and socializing. The food companies grabbed this opportunity to exert their influence on consumers. They peddled their products through free or very low cost advertising cookbooklets. Dainty, economical, and reliable recipes made from products that were pure and free of adulterants became the young housewife's new best friend. Though the recipes in these booklets were tested thoroughly by famous home economists and cooking-school experts, the dishes were the same things that women had already been preparing, with a little added convenience.

What I love most about this time period are the handwritten cookbooks that most every woman kept. They are by now in terrible shape, especially if they were ever used. You can tell what's worth cooking by the amount of food that is splattered on a particular page. When you open up one of these books, clipped recipes from newspapers drop out, some are stuck in the books with straight pins. The recipes usually have someone's name attached to them, and the handwriting is typically beautiful.

If you're lucky enough to have any of these books, hang on to them, or give them to someone who will cherish them. And while you're at it, start a cooking scrapbook with your own children.

1900-1919

※

EMMA'S CHEESE STICKS, 1913

Someone let Emma's cooking manuscript slip out of their family, and I am now the lucky owner of her wonderful collection of recipes from 1910-1930. Of little value to collectors because of its tattered and food-soiled condition, I was able to purchase the book for a song. Emma cooked with fresh heirloom vegetables from her garden and her recipes had an uncharacteristic flair to them for the time. She didn't use gelatin and other popular quick foods because (I think) she was in no hurry to get out of her kitchen.

"Chop into one cup pastry flour, a lump of butter the size of an egg, 1 cup grated cheese, a little salt, and a dash of cayenne. Add just enough ice water to mix into a ball of dough. Roll like pie crust and dot with bits of butter. Fold and roll again. Cut into strips one-inch wide and four long. Bake in a quick oven."

Author's Note: I'd omit the butter dotting after you roll it out the first time. When you roll the dough, make it thicker than you would a pie crust-about ¼ inch. Place strips on an unbuttered cookie sheet and bake in a preheated 400° oven until lightly browned. Check after about five minutes.

American involvement in WWI lasted from April 1917 until November 1918. Women in most communities across the country joined forces to send care packages to the soldiers stationed in Europe. The packages included writing supplies, handknit socks and sweaters, sewing kits, cards, chewing gum, and bible verses.

1900-1919

Skewered Coconut Shrimp

I'd like to think that if the ingredients in this dish had been available to Emma, she would have made it. I confess that I created this appetizer recently for a party and it doesn't belong in this book. But it turned out great, and I just don't care for the creamy seafood and odd meat dishes folks ate back in the early 1900s. So pardon me, and give this a try.

1 lb. large shrimp	About 30 dried apricot halves
1 red onion	¼ cup rum
1 green pepper	30 bamboo skewers soaked in water

Soak apricots in rum about 2 hours or until plump. Cut onion and pepper into 1 inch squares and peel and clean shrimp. For appetizers, use small skewers. Thread a shrimp through the head and tail, then apricot, then pepper, then onion onto each stick. Roll each skewer in coconut marinade (below) and refrigerate for 4 hours. Broil a few minutes on one side, only until vegetables begin to blacken slightly and shrimp is pink. Top with a squeeze of lime juice, chopped scallions and fresh cilantro. Serve at once.

Coconut Marinade:
Combine juice of one lime with 4 oz. unsweetened coconut milk, a tablespoon of honey, a couple tablespoons sweet chili sauce, a teaspoon grated fresh ginger, and a handful of sweetened coconut.

School Lunch Suggestions, 1915
Boys like plain folding lunch boxes, girls prefer daintiness of equipment. Always try to provide some unexpected dainty. Here are some suggestions:
- *A mashed baked bean or other sandwich*
- *Stuffed eggs with buttered rolls*
- *Individual meat or fruit turnovers*
- *Plain simple cakes like gingerbread or applesauce*

1900-1919

~

Fannie Merritt Farmer's Big Mistake

You probably have a dog-eared version of her famous 1896 Boston Cooking School cookbook on your kitchen shelf. I do. It's falling apart from all the use it had as I was learning to cook. Known as the "mother of modern measurement," I have since come to view Fannie's contribution of applying standardized measurements to popular recipes as a blot on the talents of the make-do cook.

Fannie was on the cutting edge of the Domestic Science movement in the late 19th century. Housewives were now being told by homemaking experts that not only were they providing a valuable service to their families; but they were also the caretakers of society as well. While I don't argue with this, it's just a shame that in her attempt to be more scientific about cooking, Fannie adapted recipes calling for "butter the size of an egg" to "¼ cup of butter" in the writing of her cookbook. She tampered with the folklore of cooking, and something valuable was lost in the process.

Guess how many measuring utensils I have in my kitchen. Only one: a glass cup measure, and I could do without that if I had to.

My grandmother, Maudie Smith, a wonderful make-do cook, taught me that to make a good biscuit, the dough has to look and feel a certain way and you just have to keep adjusting your ingredients until you get it right. That takes practice. Maybe Fannie thought she was doing women a favor by freeing them from the trial and error of getting their recipes just right. That took time and she thought women had more important things to tend to.

1900-1919

All my favorite cooks don't do much measuring, and they get plenty of other stuff done. My friend, Effie Price, who was born in 1914, measures the number of apples for her apple butter by the pan she cooks it in, and hers is the best you've ever tasted. If I told you what she used to do in a day as a housewife, on a mountain farm, you'd fall over from exhaustion just hearing about it.

Della Lutes writes in her 1937 book, **The Country Kitchen** (see page 21 for more on Della), "*The art of cookery in the 1870s was taught by mother to daughter, generation after generation, and each housewife knew by the artistry of touch and sight just how to measure a cupful or a pinch. It was an art.*" It still is.

Keep a Supply of Welch's in your Ice Chest

1900-1919

T his may look like a forest of battered and fried ice cream cones, but it's actually a wonderful photograph of the quintessential-early-20th-century croquette. It comes from a 1914 cookbooklet called ***Good Things to Eat Made With Bread*** from the Fleischmann Yeast Company. In this particular recipe, bread crumbs are mixed with almonds, lemon juice, milk, eggs, and butter. The mixture is shaped into "croquettes" and then rolled in egg white, dipped in more crumbs, and fried in plenty of "smoking hot fat."

Cone shaped, fried croquettes were a great way to use up bits of leftover meats, vegetables, and stale bread in the days when nothing was wasted and fat was considered nutritive because it was calorie-dense. By the 1960s, croquettes evolved into patty shapes that could be pan-fried in a little butter.

Good Things to Eat Made with Bread

John Dough raised on Fleischmann's Yeast

The Fleischmann Co.

1900-1919

SALMON CROQUETTES, 1900

I don't suggest you make this (too much fat, and not enough salmon), but this was a typical croquette recipe. The Chicken Croquettes (below) are good and you can make them with salmon.

"Mix thoroughly, roll into croquettes and fry in deep fat the following ingredients: 1 can salmon, 1 cup cold mashed potatoes, ½ cup melted butter, 2 eggs, 4 tablespoons minced onion, 2 cups bread crumbs, ½ teaspoon black pepper, ½ tsp. salt."

CHICKEN CROQUETTES, 1919

1 cup bread crumbs   2 well beaten eggs
3 cups chopped cooked chicken (ham, salmon, or turkey)

To the cooked chicken, add salt, pepper, bread crumbs and one beaten egg. If necessary, moisten with milk or chicken gravy. Shape into cones or balls, dip in bread crumbs, beaten egg, then bread crumbs. Fry until golden brown in hot fat or bake in a hot oven. **Author's note:** In addition, add ½ cup chopped onion and yellow bell pepper and a little chopped parsley. Use a scoop to shape into balls, saute in a frying pan with a little butter until lightly browned.

65 Delicious Dishes, The Fleishmann Co.

Advice from Mrs. Potter, 1910

There are four important things about a kitchen: the stove, the sink, a table, and pantry. Each one of these must be in the right place if you would save steps, for you know steps are energy and as the old saying goes, "Use your head and save your heels!"

Cupid at Home
in the Kitchen
following
Mrs. Potter's Advice

1900-1919

Roast Pork with Gingersnap Sauce

From The Settlement Cookbook: The Way to a Man's Heart, 1915.

Top slices of roast pork or baked pork chops with this sauce. Serve with thickly sliced, firm apples that have been pan sauteed and lightly sweetened.

Gingersnap Sauce:

4 ginger snaps, crushed	1 cup hot water or soup stock
½ cup brown sugar	1 lemon, sliced
¼ cup vinegar	¼ cup raisins
½ tsp. onion juice (a little grated onion will do)	

Mix all together and cook until smooth. It must taste strong of vinegar and sugar and more of either may be added to suit taste. Grated gingerbread may be used in place of the gingersnaps.

Fresh Corn and Sweet Potato Scallop

4 large ears of boiled corn
4 large sweet potatoes

"Cut off the corn and slice the potatoes. Fill alternately into a baking dish. Brown a tablespoonful of butter, and a tablespoon flour in a small pan. Add one cup of cold water or milk. Cook five minutes, stirring until thick. Add salt and pepper. Pour over the corn and potatoes and bake 20 minutes."

"No Oil to Soil"

"We offer you whole and appetizing dishes, easily, quickly, and economically made which we believe will be of interest to the progressive and prudent housewife."

The Fleischmann Yeast Company 1919

1900-1919

~

HANNAH'S MOLASSES GINGER CAKES, 1910

These are just too good. Big, soft, spicy, and old-fashioned. My teenage son is hooked on these and makes them frequently.

1 cup molasses
¾ cup sugar
¾ cup butter, melted
½ cup evaporated milk
1 Tbs. lemon rind or ¾ tsp. lemon extract (or both)
Flour to make a stiff dough (about 4 cups)

1 tsp. soda
1 Tbs. ginger
1 tsp. cinnamon

Combine molasses, butter, sugar, soda and spices, and mix well. Add milk and lemon rind or lemon extract. Beat well. Add four cups flour and refrigerate your dough until it's firm enough to roll out. (I'm impatient, so I stick it in the freezer for 20 minutes.) Roll dough out on a floured board about one inch thick and cut with a round biscuit cutter. Bake in a preheated 350° oven until lightly browned—about 12 minutes.

The Great Molasses Flood of 1919

Here's why you shouldn't store 2.5 million gallons of molasses in a 50 foot high tank in the middle of a big city like Boston. Back in 1919, molasses was a popular sweetener for baking as well as brewing, especially in Boston. The sticky sweetener was made in factories and stored in large tanks near the harbor. Some say that an unseasonably warm day on January 15 caused molasses expansion and the ensuing explosion that killed 21 people and injured 150. The 20 foot wall of molasses also killed horses and destroyed homes, warehouses, and the train line. The clean-up took 6 months; and it's said that the sidewalks oozed molasses for 30 years.

1900-1919

Culinary Heresy

I have no idea who authored the little book called **Quick Cooking: A Book of Culinary Heresies** from the turn of the 20th century; but I can sure tell you that she was a rebellious woman. She wasn't about to waste her valuable time in the kitchen preparing the laborious, cooking-school dishes that were popular in her day. This author rose up and spoke for the women she knew when she said:

> *"The editor assumes that **Quick Cooking** will be consulted chiefly by tired and overworked wives and mothers, who constitute by far the larger number of the housekeepers of the land."*

A woman born too soon, she encouraged housewives to *"demand shelled peas, string beans, and lima beans ready for the pot, fish ready- cleaned, fowls cleaned and trussed for the oven"* from their food dealers. Why, this housewife had just about had enough! How should women spend their time, you ask?

"Going to town to attend to business or professional duties; taking in a round of shopping, sitting down to the sewing-machine, spending the afternoon with an invalid friend, or seeking needed recreation."

The book is divided into three sections: Quickest Dishes, 5-15 minutes, 20 minutes or more, and Black List. The latter are dishes that your husband may demand and "must be accepted by the overburdened housewife as necessary crosses to bear."

To tell you the truth, most of her recipes aren't very good by today's standards, but she had the right idea: fresh ingredients, cooked lightly, and seasoned well. I just can't get excited about Breaded Frog's Saddles and Tongue Toast. However, this cherry dish on the next page is pretty darn good.

1900-1919

～

CHERRY PUDDING SHORT-CAKE, 1900

A cherry cobbler from the author of **Quick Cooking** *(see story left.)*

"Stone ripe cherries, squeezing the stones out by pinching the fruit between thumb and forefinger, if a good cherry-stoner is not at hand, being careful to catch all the juice that escapes. Add three quarters the weight of sugar and simmer on the stove for fifteen minutes. Make ready a thick batter prepared as for short-cake. Spread this over the top of the pan in which the cherries are cooking, set in the oven and bake to a golden brown. Send to the table inverted and serve with cream."

Here's how the author would have prepared this dish if only she could have:

 1 can sour pitted cherries   2 level Tbs. corn starch
 1 cup sugar

Cook together, stirring constantly until bubbly and clear. Pour into a buttered skillet or casserole dish. Cover with shortcake:

 2 cups flour   ¾ tsp. salt
 ½ cup butter   ½ cup sugar
 3 tsp. baking powder   Milk

Mix flour with baking powder, sugar, and salt. Cut butter into the dry ingredients and add enough milk to make a stiff dough that you can roll out. Roll dough the same size as your baking dish and place on top of the hot cherries. Bake in a preheated 375° oven about 20 minutes until shortcake is lightly browned and cooked through. Loosen edges and invert onto a pan to serve. Or, just serve from the baking dish...the author would have liked that!

1900-1919

EGGLESS, MILKLESS, BUTTERLESS CAKE, 1917

*This recipe comes from Royal Baking Powder's book **55 Ways to Save Eggs**. Saving eggs (which had become scarce and expensive) meant substituting one teaspoon baking powder per egg called for in a recipe. In this dandy little book, directions for the old way are given alongside the ones for the new way. I vote for the old way, personally, and recommend using just a pinch of nutmeg instead of a teaspoon.*

Old Way

*½ cup butter
1 cup brown sugar
*2 eggs
*1 cup milk
1 cup raisins
2 oz. citron, cut fine
2 cups flour
*2 tsp. Royal baking powder
1 tsp. nutmeg
1 tsp. cinnamon
½ tsp. salt

*Substitutions were made for these
 ingredients in the "New Way."

New Way

Substitute the following for starred ingredients, left.

½ cup shortening
No eggs
1¾ cups water
5 tsp. Royal baking powder

55 Ways to Save Eggs

Directions:
Boil sugar, liquid, fruit, shortening, salt, and spices together in a saucepan for 3 minutes. When cool, add flour and baking powder which have been sifted together. Mix well, bake in a loaf pan in moderate (350°) oven 45 minutes and top with white icing made from confectioners sugar, butter, vanilla, and milk.

1900-1919

Photo courtesy of the State Historical Society of Wisconsin

MOCK CHERRY PIE, 1915

Anytime I see a "mock" recipe in an old cookbook, I take a closer look. These recipes are the hallmark of an inventive cook who was not going to let seasonal scarcity get in the way of her good cookin'. Almost all mock recipes are good and this one is no exception. This pie does taste surprisingly like cherries. It has a great texture and the bright red filling looks wonderful peeking through a lattice crust. Serve it with vanilla ice cream or whipped cream.

2 cups fresh cranberries	2 Tbs. corn starch
1¼ cup sugar	Juice & rind ½ lemon
½ cup cold water	1 cup raisins
1 apple cut fine	½ tsp. vanilla

Dissolve corn starch in water. Add to cranberries and raisins and cook until cranberries burst and mixture turns translucent. Add lemon juice, rind, sugar, apple, and vanilla and stir well. Pour into an unbaked pie shell and top with lattice crust. Bake at 350° until filling bubbles and crust is nicely browned (30-40 minutes.)

1920's

decade of prosperity, conservatism, social radicalism, youth, and technology; the 1920's had it all. Following on the heels of the passing of the 19th amendment, giving women the right to vote, young mothers and wives now had better things to do than hang around the house all day. They bobbed their hair, slimmed their hips, and donned WWI aviator clothes. With prohibition came the cocktail party; couples entertained in their homes and offered their guests mixed drinks and canapes that were intended to cover the strong taste of homemade liquor.

Vitamins were largely discovered in the 1920's. Products containing these new nutrients were the ones that made it onto the grocer's crowded shelves. By the end of the decade, most American families owned an automobile, a radio, and a bevy of appliances designed to save women time spent in housekeeping and cooking tasks. Bridge parties, picnics, volunteering, college, and jobs outside the home were waiting.

Advertising cookbooks from the 1920s provide a vivid picture of the conflicting societal expectations that women from this time period faced. On one hand, there is this quote from a 1926 Watkins products cookbook:

> *"Woman certainly deserves better than to be sacrificed to that nightmarish horror of pots, pans and plans, which steals away the joy from the whole day, each mealtime."*

And then you have these oppressive poems found in a 1927 Hays, Kansas cookbook:

*Serve your husband what he likes
and save a hundred household strikes.*

*He criticized her pudding,
He grumbled at her cake.
But she won him with her doughnuts
Like his mother used to make.*

1920's

For the most part, the recipes from the 1920's were still made-from-scratch good. Though electric refrigerators were available by 1925, they were expensive. Most homes still had an icebox or in rural areas, a spring box. Housewives shopped for fresh produce and meat every couple of days. A limited variety of ingredients was available, so meals were wholesome and uncomplicated.

The Psalm of Wife

Lives of icemen keep us wishing,
That the summer days were o'er.
When departing, they leave behind them,
Foot prints on the kitchen floor!

1920's

Asparagus and Shrimp Salad

*This recipe comes from a 1920s cookbook called **New Calendar of Salads: 365 answers to the daily question "What shall we have for salad?"** On March 15th, this is the salad you should have.*

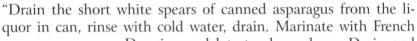

"Drain the short white spears of canned asparagus from the liquor in can, rinse with cold water, drain. Marinate with French Dressing and let stand one hour. Drain and arrange in a wreath of small crisp lettuce heart-leaves. Remove the intestinal veins from one cup of fresh cooked or canned shrimp. Mince them and mix thoroughly with one cup of mayonnaise dressing thinned with ¼ cup cream. Pour over prepared asparagus. Chill and serve at Lenten Luncheon."

Recipe Update: Steam fresh asparagus, marinate in vinegarette dressing of your choice. Place drained asparagus on lettuce leaves (divide into individual servings). Place a pile of small, cooked shrimp on top of the asparagus and drizzle with a mixture of mayonnaise and lemon juice (or just lemon.) Sprinkle chopped green onions on top.

A waffle, a muffin, and a gem
We wish you luck with all of them.

If nature did not give you that which is yours by right
Just nibble at these dainties to give you an appetite.

Golden fluffy biscuits buttered from the pan
Are bound to appease the children and please most any man.

1920's

W hile poring through early advertising booklets, I came upon the **Presto Book of Menus and Recipes** (for home-canned foods), written by Della Thompson Lutes for the Cupples Company in 1929. My heart was immediately captured by the uncomplicated words of a contented woman I felt I'd known all my life. In her writing, she speaks of women as the moving spirit of the home, and of the kitchen as "one of the loveliest spots therein where the work done is a pleasure (since times have changed and women are there by choice)."

My curiosity about this delightful woman led me to an on-line purchase of her book that's been long out of print entitled "**The Country Kitchen.**" Even MORE wonderful is Della's reminiscence of her life as a 6-year-old growing up in rural Michigan in 1870. *"The kitchen was by all odds the most important room of the house. There Mother cooked and Father got in the way."* The book is punctu-

ated with family recipes and stories of favorite foods like this one for Riz Biscuits (known to us now as Angel Biscuits.) I've adapted this recipe to suit the 21st century cook.

Riz Biscuits

2½ cups self-rising flour
1/3 cup shortening
¼ cup sugar

1 package yeast
Pinch baking soda
1 cup buttermilk

Rub the shortening into the flour. Stir in sugar. In a separate bowl, sprinkle yeast and soda into lukewarm buttermilk. Add the liquids to the dry ingredients and combine. Turn out onto a floured board and knead for a minute, adding flour if necessary to make a soft dough. Roll out to ½ inch thickness, cut with a biscuit cutter, and place on a buttered baking sheet to rise for 30 minutes to one hour. Bake in a 400° oven until lightly browned.
Author's Note: Buttermilk is a must for this recipe.

1920's

A Delicious Breakfast Dish, 1929

"A set of fresh brains scalded to remove the tissue covering. When nicely dressed, cut into pieces the size of large oysters, then salt and pepper and roll in meal or rolled cracker crumbs. Fry in boiling hot lard a rich brown. Fine. Try it!"

...Or not!

Chicken Pot Pie With Sweet Potato Crust

3 cups diced boiled chicken
1 cup sliced carrots
1 onion, chopped
1 Tbs. fresh parsley

½ cup whole milk
1 cup chicken broth
2 Tbs. flour
Salt and Pepper to taste

Boil the water you cooked your chicken in down to one cup, set aside. Place chicken and vegetables in a casserole dish. Add 2 Tbs. flour to a little milk, making a smooth paste. Whisk in the rest of milk and chicken broth. Cook over medium heat until thickened. Season with salt and pepper. Pour over chicken and vegetables and top with crust (see below). Bake in a 350° oven until crust is lightly browned and the insides are bubbly.

Sweet Potato Crust:

1 cup flour
1 tsp. baking powder
½ tsp. salt

1 cup mashed sweet potatoes
¼ cup butter

Mix flour, baking powder, and salt. Cut in butter. Add enough sweet potato until you have a mixture you can "work." Roll out the size of your casserole dish.

1920's

Apple and Ham Casserole

3 apples
3 sweet potatoes, cooked whole
6 servings cooked sliced ham

1 tsp. dry mustard
¼ cup water or apple juice
4 Tbs. brown sugar

Peel, core, and slice apples in rounds. Arrange apple rounds, sliced sweet potatoes and ham in layers in a greased casserole dish ending with apple rounds. Sprinkle each layer with mustard. Add water or apple juice; cover and bake 50 minutes in a moderate (350°) oven or until apples are tender. Remove cover, top with brown sugar and bake about 10 minutes longer. (You can substitute maple syrup for the brown sugar and cooked and drained sausage for the ham.)

This is a baked, spiced ham from 1927, turned sideways. If you listen carefully, you can hear it hooting softly. Just watch it fly off your plate!

What Goes With What, 1927

With roast beef serve horseradish.
With roast mutton serve currant jelly.
With broiled mutton serve caper sauce.
With roast pork serve apple sauce.
With roast lamb serve mint sauce.
With roast turkey serve cranberries.
With roast duck serve currant jelly.
With mackerel serve gooseberries.
With roast goose serve apple sauce.

1920's

Y ou wouldn't believe how difficult it is to find interesting recipes from the early 20th century that people would actually prepare today. Well, I hit pay dirt when I found *"How Mama Could Cook"* in an antique booth. Written by Dorothy Malone in 1946, the book chronicles the life of her feminist, defiant, rather flamboyant mother with perky stories and recipes that will blow you away. You know how you buy a cookbook and hope for one recipe that you'll prepare regularly; well just about every one in this book is worth making, and the only thing you'll have to go out and get is a varied selection of liquors.

Mama threw wine, sherry, champagne, Cointreau, brandy, or rum into everything she cooked. There are recipes for making brandy and wine in the book, so her cooking probably didn't suffer much during the period of prohibition. I put her recipes in this chapter as an act of anti-temperance-movement defiance in Mama's honor.

MAMA'S LEAVE THEM SMILING CANTALOUPE

"Cut the meat from a cantaloupe, sweeten it with old-fashioned rock candy ground to powder with a rolling pin and make it wicked with ¼ cup dark rum. Leave it to ripen in the icebox, then serve in sherbet glasses."

STRAWBERRY CHANTILLY

"Hull and sweeten a quart of strawberries, ply them with 4 tablespoons of cherry brandy or Cointreau and chill thoroughly. Then mix them through a quart of vanilla ice cream which Mama would let melt until it got to the swirly stage."

1920's

Raisin and Nut Stuffed Apples

I *just made this dish and it's unbelievably delicious. Sort of a meatless mincemeat in an apple. It helps to use a melon baller to scoop out the pulp.*

One baking apple per person	Brown Sugar
Chopped almonds or pecans	Raisins
Grated lemon peel	Dark rum

Cut the top off each apple, take out core with small end of melon baller and discard. Scoop out apple pulp to within a half inch of the skin. Chop the apple pulp fine and add other ingredients. (Now, you don't need me to tell you how much, just throw in what tastes good to you.) Add enough rum to make a "workable mixture." Spoon the mixture back into the apples. Put the apples in a casserole dish, then add a little water around the apples. Cover with foil and bake 45 minutes at 350° until apples are tender. Spoon the liquid left in the pan over the apples before serving.

Brandied Bananas

"Sometimes, Mama would put bananas in a baking dish, dot each one with butter and dust it with sugar. Put to bake at 350°, she would turn them once, and when soft and golden, she would pour warmed apple brandy over them, lighting it as she brought the dish to the table. With them she served either vanilla ice cream or sweetened whipped cream."

1920's

Mama's Chocolate Risin' Cake

1 cup shortening	¼ cup lukewarm water
2 cups sugar	2¼ cups sifted cake flour
3 eggs, separated	½ tsp. salt
3 oz. baking chocolate	1 tsp. soda
1 cup milk	3 Tbs. hot water
1 pkg. yeast	4 Tbs. rum

"Cream the shortening and add the sugar, creaming again. Then add the melted chocolate, the milk, and the yeast which has been mixed with the warm water. Sift the flour and salt together, beat into the mixture gradually.

Now cover the bowl, set in as warm a corner as you have, and let it sit over night. Next morning, dissolve the soda in the hot water, and stir into the cake. Blend in the egg yolks and rum. Beat the egg whites stiff, and fold them gently into the batter. Pour the batter into greased and floured cake pans, 9-inch size. Bake at 350° for 25 minutes."

Mama frosts the cake:
"Shake the layers out of the pan on waxed paper, and when cool, put the bottom layer on your cake dish. Spread rum-laced apricot preserves over the first layer, then add the top layer and spread with your favorite chocolate icing."

1920's

THE PERFECT CAKE

Women living in the 1920s and 30s must have had cake anxiety if you believe what the "make a better cake" cookbooks say. The road to the perfect cake was paved with so many required characteristics. Here's a score card for judging cakes from the **1928 Swans Down's Cake Manual**:

General Appearance (Shape 5%, Size 5%, Crust 10%)	20%
Flavor (Odor, Taste)	35%
Lightness	15%
Crumb (Texture 20%, Color 5%, Distribution of gas, 5%)	30%
Total	100%

1920's

AUNT SAMMY'S GINGERBREAD WITH CREAM CHEESE FILLING

From a booklet called **Aunt Sammy's Radio Recipes** *"issued to meet the enormous demand for printed copies of the most popular recipes broadcast from October 1926 to June 1927, on the Housekeeper's Chat programs of the radio service, USDA." This book is easy to find, and it is a gem. No wiggly, weird, instant foods. Just good, time-tested, wholesome, tasty, and creative dishes.*

Before you start: People didn't eat their food spicy in the 1920's, so I've increased the cinnamon and ginger and added nutmeg instead of cloves. Stir the liquids into the dry ingredients until well blended and pour into an 8 by 10-inch baking dish that's been well buttered. Bake about 30 minutes. I have no idea what two cream cheeses means in the Cheese Filling recipe; just use an 8 oz. package of Neufchatel (reduced fat) cheese.

Gingerbread:

1 cup milk	3 teaspoons baking powder
1 cup molasses	3 cups soft wheat white flour
½ cup butter	½ tsp. salt
1 egg	1 teaspoon ginger
½ teaspoon soda	½ tsp. nutmeg
½ cup sugar	1 teaspoon cinnamon

"Mix the dry ingredients. Stir the liquid into the dry ingredients. For a shallow loaf, the oven should be moderate, about 375°."

Cheese Filling:

2 Neufchatel or cream cheeses	1 cup chopped nuts
2 cups chopped dates	pinch salt

Mash the cheese and mix with it enough cream to give it the consistency of a soft filling. Add the dates, nuts, salt, and mix well. Split open a thick loaf of hot gingerbread, spread the cheese mixture on the lower half, replace the upper part and press it down lightly. The quantity of cheese filling given here is enough for a pan of gingerbread about 8 by 10 inches. Serve the gingerbread while still hot.

1920's

Want Health and Happiness?
Get a Refrigerator!

"To many people electric refrigeration is still such a novelty that they scarcely realize the range of its possibilities. It is almost like having an Aladdin's lamp and not knowing the right way to rub it. With a General Electric Refrigerator, simple recipes, easily prepared, produce delightful results. The owning of such a refrigerator is a form of health and happiness insurance which every homemaker in America should have the privilege of enjoying."

G.E. Electric Refrigerator Recipes, 1927

BUTTERSCOTCH ICEBOX COOKIES

½ cup butter
1 cup brown sugar
1 egg
1 tsp. vanilla

2 cups flour
1 tsp. baking powder
½ cup chopped nuts

Cream butter and sugar, add egg and vanilla and mix well. Mix baking powder with flour and add to creamed mixture. Stir in nuts. Roll in waxed paper and refrigerate until firm. Storing them in the freezer works well, too. (That wasn't an option with G.E.'s 1927 refrigerator.) Slice and bake 8 minutes or until lightly browned in a preheated 375° oven.

1930's

Y ou may think of the 1930s as the decade of the Great Depression, but many remember it as a time when the pace of life slowed, and nothing was taken for granted. Families shared what little they had with their needier neighbors. It was a time of church suppers, picnics at the lake, get-togethers with friends and family, recipe-sharing, making-do, and doing without.

Feed bags, bleached and washed were transformed into sheets, pajamas, and underwear for the family. Printed feed sacks became lively quilts, dresses and men's shirts. Everything was saved and re-used. A 1931 Bond Bread Book encouraged "far-sighted women to keep a crumb jar in the icebox so they need not ever feel guilty again of throwing away a piece of Bond bread."

Most of the recipes and poems in this chapter come from Lucy's recipe scrapbook, a treasure I found at a local auction that was the inspiration for this book. Some of her recipes came from friends and family, and others were clipped from newspapers and magazines. Several were given to her at cooking seminars taught by well-known home economists of her time. I must say there's nothing special about most of Lucy's recipes, but she was obviously a warm, artistic, family woman who loved her lot in life. I wish I could just once go back in time and eat dinner at her table.

1930's

LUCY'S RUSSIAN TEA

½ cup orange pekoe tea
3 cups sugar
Juice of 3 lemons
Juice of 3 oranges
1 tsp. cinnamon
1 tsp. nutmeg
1 tsp. cloves

Pour 1 quart of boiling water over the tea. Tie spices in a muslin or cheesecloth bag and add to tea with the sugar and juices. Let stand three hours. Strain and add one gallon of either cold or boiling water. (I recommend ½ tsp. each nutmeg and cloves and 1 tsp. cinnamon).
"Rena served to sewing circle. Good."

SPIKED CIDER CUP

I don't think Lucy actually made this punch with liquor. Next to the ingredient gin in the recipe, she wrote, 1-2 pints?? I'll bet she misread ½ as 1-2, or maybe she just gave wild parties!

Juice of 4 oranges and 2 lemons
½ Gallon apple cider
1 quart ginger ale
½ pint gin
Slices of oranges, and pineapple will improve flavor.

A Song About Kettles

BY NANCY BYRD TURNER

Life is full of changes,
Years are hard and long;
But the world's teakettles
Keep their old song.

The same good humming
That they've hummed,
   nights and days,
Since a woman set the
   first one
Over a blaze.

Oh, the long pleasure
Their music has been
To calm cats purring
With their paws folded in;

To gray grandmothers
In the twilight sitting,
Feet on a cricket;
Hands full of knitting.

To children nodding
At the edge of a dream,
Their heads all misty
In a silver steam!

Time, change, weather-
None of those things
Can make much trouble
When a teakettle sings!

1930's

❧

Lucy's Oysters for Goodness Sake

　1 pint oysters, drained
　12 slices thick bacon, cut in quarters
　Toothpicks (about 25) soaked in water 30 minutes

Arrange each oyster between two pieces of bacon on a toothpick. Place in a pan and sprinkle with pepper. Broil about three minutes, then turn and broil the other side until bacon is crisp. Serve at once.

𝒦ELVINATOR truly adds glamor and romance to homemaking! It takes the nerve racking rush out of big dinners and the every day grind out of small ones. And, it is within reach of all.

1930's

Parker House Rolls

Said to have been invented accidentally by a chef at Boston's famous Parker House Hotel in 1870, there are countless variations of this roll recipe. The one thing they all have in common is that the dough is rolled, cut, buttered, and folded over to give the rolls that celebrated shape. This recipe was collected by Lucy.

2 cups warm milk
1 pkg. yeast
2 tsp. salt

2 Tbs. sugar
4 Tbs. butter, softened
Flour (about 4 cups)

Dissolve yeast in milk. Stir in salt, sugar, and butter. Add flour until you have a dough you can work. Knead dough until it's elastic then shape into a ball. Let the dough rise in a buttered bowl with a towel on top about an hour or until doubled in bulk. Punch down, and roll the dough out ½ inch thick onto a floured surface. Cut with biscuit cutter. Brush tops with butter, then fold over, lightly pinching edges. Place on a greased cookie sheet and let rise about 45 minutes. Bake in a preheated 400° oven 10-15 minutes until lightly browned.

Are You an Up-To-Date Housewife?

Shopping tours, bridge parties, club meetings! How many activities there are to fill the days of the up-to-date housewife!

The wise and efficient homemaker is in a state of constant preparedness, for she knows that cans of ready to serve foods will keep indefinitely and provide that feeling of security that is invaluable.
Heinz, 57 Unusual Ways to Serve Spaghetti, 1933

1930's

Vegetable Pie with Cheese Biscuit Topping

2 large potatoes, diced	1 medium onion, sliced
3 stalks celery, chopped	2 cups seasoned white sauce
2 carrots, sliced	Cheese biscuit topping

Simmer vegetables until done, reserve cooking liquid. Make white sauce with 2 Tbs. each flour and melted butter, 2 cloves garlic, 1 cup milk and 1 cup vegetable liquid. (Saute garlic in butter, add flour and cook a few minutes. Add liquids slowly and cook until thickened.)

Cheese Biscuit Topping:

2 cups self-rising flour	Buttermilk (½ to ¾ cup)
5 Tbs. butter	1 cup grated cheddar cheese

Work butter into flour, then add half of cheese. Add buttermilk until you have a soft dough you can roll out. Roll out ½ inch thick on a floured surface and cut with biscuit cutter. Place biscuits on top of vegetable mixture and top with remaining cheese. Bake in a preheated 375° oven until mixture bubbles and biscuits are lightly browned. You can throw cooked chicken or any other vegetables into the pie before baking.

Orange Harvard Beets

1 lb. cooked, sliced beets	¼ cup vinegar
1 Tbs. cornstarch	Juice of an orange
¼ cup sugar (or less)	Salt and pepper to taste

Combine all ingredients except beets and cook until thickened. Add beets and heat through. Dot with butter before serving.

1930's

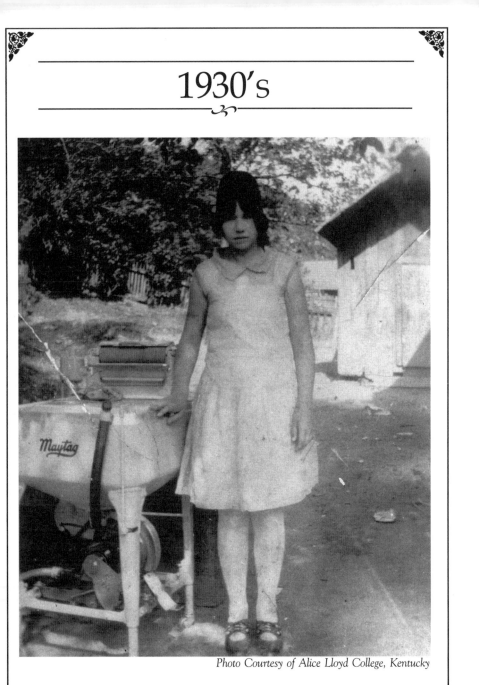

Photo Courtesy of Alice Lloyd College, Kentucky

This One Does it All!

This versatile 1930s Maytag washing machine could be powered either by gasoline or electricity. Optional attachments were available that could be used to grind meat and churn either butter or ice cream.

1930's

❧

Weird Noodle Dishes, 1933

"How to Become Famous For Your Spaghetti Dishes"

"Fifty-seven unusual ways to serve spaghetti...surely, no housewife will want to neglect this important source of tasty, nourishing dinners. The recipes feature delicious, economical Heinz Cooked Spaghetti." You too, could become famous (as in, "She cooks the weirdest spaghetti!") if you prepare these tasty canned spaghetti dishes.

> **Spaghetti Caruso (chicken livers smothered in spaghetti)**
> **Cooked Spaghetti with Frankfurters**
> **Spaghetti and Egg Scramble**
> **Steak Stuffed with Spaghetti**
> Heinz 57 Unusual Ways to Serve Spaghetti, 1933

For the
CHILDREN
...tasty and nutritious recipes

Suggested dishes for youngsters from Mueller's 1933 Noodle Cookbook:

> **Egg Noodles with Prunes**
> **Egg Noodles with Spinach**
> **Elbow Macaroni with Liver**
> **Egg Noodles with Frankfurters and Sauerkraut**
> **Egg Noodles with Tongue**

1930's
～

LUCY'S CHOCOLATE PUDDING

People don't have to make their own pudding any-more since there's cook and serve, instant, and pre-packaged individual servings to choose from. But there's nothing like good-old-homemade pudding without polysorbate 60, artificial flavors and dyes. We make this all the time when we're in the mood for puddingy comfort food. Serve warm with whipped cream.

2/3 cup sugar	2½ cups milk
1/3 cup cocoa	1 egg, if desired
3 Tbs. corn starch	1 tsp. vanilla
½ tsp. salt	1 Tbs. butter

"Mix dry ingredients in heavy sauce pan; gradually stir in milk. Cook over low heat, stirring constantly until mixture thickens. Mix in lightly beaten egg; return and cook with continual stirring 'til mixture again thickens. Stir in vanilla and butter."

Photo Courtesy of Library of Congress

1930's

OLD-FASHIONED RAISIN FILLED ELECTRIC APPLIANCE COOKIES

How exciting to be able to cook with electricity! This recipe was tested and approved by The Edison Friendly Kitchen some time in the 1930s. These cookies are good!

¾ cup butter
1 cup sugar
1 egg
1 tsp. vanilla

¼ cup milk
3 cups flour
2 tsp. baking powder
Pinch salt

"Cream butter and sugar. Add egg and beat. Pour in milk and vanilla. Combine dry ingredients and add to creamed mixture. Chill thoroughly in *electric refrigerator*. Divide dough into 4 parts and roll each out into same-size rectangles about ¼-inch thick. Place two rectangles on parchment paper and spread half of raisin filling on each. Top with remaining dough rectangles, even the edges up. If you have a pastry wheel, cut the dough about half way through into individual pieces. Use a fork to prick a couple holes in each piece. Bake in a 375° *electric range oven* for 15 minutes."

Filling:
1½ cup raisins, chopped
½ cup sugar
2 Tbs. flour

1 Tbs. lemon juice
¾ cup hot water
Pinch salt

"Cook ingredients together over medium heat of *electric range* until mixture thickens, stirring almost constantly to prevent burning. Cool before using in cookies."

1930's

Toll House Cookies, 1939

*Toll House Cookies were acciden-
tally invented in 1930 by Ruth
Wakefield, who ran the Toll House
Inn in Whitman, Massachusetts.
She was making chocolate cookies,
ran out of Baker's chocolate, and
added a diced Nestle's Semisweet
chocolate bar to her dough. Ruth
figured the chocolate would melt
and mix in with the dough, but we
all know it didn't. Well, the cookies
were a hit and she made a deal
with Nestle where they could print her recipe on their chocolate bar in
return for a lifetime supply of chocolate. In 1939, Nestle began making
scored chocolate bars packaged with a nifty chopper. Here's a dough-smeared
recipe card from the late 1930s with the Toll House Cookie recipe cut from
a Nestle's Semi-Sweet Chocolate Bar.*

𝕿oll 𝕳ouse CHOCOLATE COOKIES

FROM THE FAMOUS NEW ENGLAND INN

Cream
1 cup butter, add
¾ cup brown sugar
¾ cup granulated sugar and
2 eggs beaten whole. Dissolve
1 tsp. soda in
1 tsp. hot water, and mix alternately with
2¼ cups flour sifted with
1 tsp. salt. Lastly add
1 cup chopped nuts and

2 Economy size bars (7 oz. ea.)
   Nestlé's Semi-Sweet
   Chocolate which have been
   cut in pieces the size of a pea.
   Flavor with
1 tsp. vanilla and drop by half
   teaspoons on a greased
   cookie sheet. Bake 10 to 12
   minutes in 375° oven.
   Makes 100 cookies.

NOTE:—Do not melt chocolate. Cut along scores—pieces are
the proper size. Chocolate cuts easily at room temperature.

1930's

~~

A Page From Lucy's Recipe Scrapbook

MY KITCHEN

Here I may be a scientist
  Who measures as she makes.
Here I may be an artist
  Creating as she bakes.
Here busy heart and brain and hand
  May feel and think and do.
A kitchen is a happy place
  To make a dream come true.

**PUT ME
IN YOUR PANTRY**
_ if you want
better meals

Sunny Peach Pie

<u>Combine</u>, ¼ cup sugar and 3 Tbs. cornstarch.

<u>Add</u>, 1 cup of syrup, drained from one 2 cup can sliced peaches.

<u>Cook</u> until thick, stirring constantly. Remove from heat.

<u>Add</u> ¼ cup fresh orange juice and 1 tsp. grated rind, 1 Tbs. butter, pinch salt. Blend into peaches.

Turn into a cooked and cooled pastry shell and chill.

1930's

Miss Bryant's Fruit Confection

This is a cookie bar version of the popular uncooked fruit cake that was a favorite of recipe exchangers in the 1930s. "Dot" chocolate referred to semi-sweet chocolate.

Equal parts figs, dates, nuts, and raisins. Grind or chop fine and moisten with lemon juice. Press into a pan. Let stand until firm and cut into squares. Dip in melted "Dot" chocolate.

Apricot Coconut Bars

Crust: 1 cup flour   ½ cup oats
                ¼ cup sugar   ½ cup butter
Cut butter into dry ingredients. Press into a 9 inch square baking pan. Bake at 350° until lightly browned.

Filling: 1/3 cup flour   2 eggs
                ½ tsp. baking powder   ½ cup brown sugar
                ¼ tsp. salt   1 cup flaked coconut
                1 cup dried apricots   1 tsp. almond extract
Dice apricots and simmer five minutes in a little water. Drain, and let cool. Sift together baking powder, salt, and flour. Beat eggs and add sugar and extract. Add dry ingredients, the apricots, and half the coconut and mix well. Spread onto the crust, sprinkle with remaining coconut, and bake at 350° about 25 minutes. When cool, cut into bars.

1940's

*U*se it up, wear it out, make it do, or do without! was the rallying cry heard from those left to care for the American home front during WWII. When I asked my mother, Nancy Smith Swell, to share with me memories of her life as a teenager growing up in her rural, Salem, West Virginia hometown during the war from 1941-1945, she had this to say:

"Mom made all my clothes, we did have our clothes washed at the Empire Laundry. I still remember their coloring books. It was the first time I ever saw colors appear with water. Shoes were rationed as well; three pairs a year were allowed."

"Though Victory Gardens were grown on every speck of available space, just about everybody in Salem already grew their own vegetables. There was a special effort to can food, to save rationed goods for the boys overseas. Everyone was involved in the war effort. Every able-bodied man went. Well, one fellow I knew said he couldn't fight in the war because he said, "I got the illitracy and thar ain't no cure.""

"Canned vegetables, meat, sugar, coffee, butter, and more were rationed. My dad had a grocery store and he kept the sugar coupons in the bank. He used to fuss because sugar came in 100 pound bags, and he could never get 20 five-pound bags out of it. Everyone had their groceries delivered, because there was no gasoline. We had the same gas allotment as the coal truck drivers. I drove the delivery truck and ate at customer's houses all over town."

Most of the recipes in this chapter reflect the struggles faced by women during wartime as they coped with food shortages, worked in defense positions outside the home, preserved their own food, raised their families, keeping their patriotic spirit alive all the while.

Nancy Swell 1942

1940's

POPOVERS

*I just love appliance cookbooks. This recipe is from **Electric Cooking With Your Hotpoint Automatic Range**. All the graphics on this page are from this book. Have you ever seen anyone so excited about cooking electric oven meals for her family?*

1 cup sifted flour
½ tsp. salt
2 eggs
1 cup whole milk

"Combine ingredients in the order given and beat until all flour is dampened. Beat with rotary or electric beater for 2 minutes. Fill greased custard cups one third full (you can use a muffin tin). Bake at 400° for about 40 minutes. Serve immediately with butter and jam or fill with chicken salad. Makes 8 large popovers."

1940's

⸙

Lumpy Soup

This was a delicious and inexpensive filling dish that many Americans of Eastern European descent fed their families during hard times. Rivels, also called spaetzle, are little egg noodle dumplings dropped into boiling broth and cooked until they float to the top. If you're in a hurry, dried spaetzle is available in most grocery stores; but homemade is always better!

2 onions sliced thinly	2 Tbs. butter
5 cups beef or chicken broth	1 large potato, diced

Melt the butter and saute the onions until golden and soft. Add the stock, salt and pepper to taste, and simmer about 20 minutes. Press the rivel batter through a colander (or a ricer) into the soup. Or, you can quickly drop tiny bits from a spoon into the broth. Boil until rivels rise to the surface.

Rivels: 2 cups flour 1 or 2 eggs
1 tsp. salt ¾ cup milk

Photo by Gideon Laney, Courtesy of David Anderson

Home Delivery

Items that were commonly delivered to the home doorstep until the 1960's included:

Milk
Dairy Products
Juice
Eggs
Bread
Ice Cream

1940's

Aunt Mary's Beef Stroganoff

Beef tenderloins were rationed during the war, so dishes like this didn't reappear until the late 1940s. My Aunt Mary from Athens, West Virginia loved to cook, and this is her recipe.

1 large chopped onion	1 cup brown sauce
1 garlic bud, chopped	½ cup sour cream
2 cups sliced, fresh mushrooms	¼ cup sherry wine
1 lb. beef tenderloin tips cut in strips or sliced	

In a skillet, heat a little oil or meat drippings. Toss in tenderloin strips. Use a high flame, stir occasionally. When brown, remove and discard most of the fat, leaving just enough to cook onions and mushrooms. Simmer a few minutes. Toss in sherry and brown sauce. Then beat in sour cream and bring just to boiling stage. Add meat and blend well. Pour over cooked wide noodles topped with snipped chives.

Author's Note: What is brown sauce? I have no idea. I haven't eaten beef since 1974. It's probably gravy made from what's left in the pan after cooking the meat. So I would add ¾ cup water to the drippings along with the sherry and cook a few minutes until your sauce is brown.

WARTIME-RATION RECIPES FOR DELICIOUS MEALS

World War II Posters

- *That tired feeling. Rx: regular rest and sleep, good food, recreation.*
- *Food is a weapon, don't waste it. Buy wisely, cook carefully, eat it all.*
- *You can use the land you have to grow the food you need.*
- *For work, for play, 2 squares a day: eat the basic 7 way.*
- *Save waste fats for explosives, take them to your meat dealer.*
- *Riding alone is like riding with Hitler!*
- *Longing won't get him back sooner. Get a war job!*
- *I'm as patriotic as can be, and ration points won't worry me!*

1940's

~

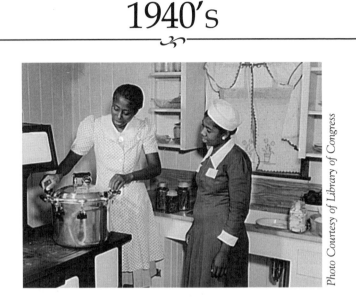

Photo Courtesy of Library of Congress

VOLCANO POTATOES

If you want a book that reflects WWII cookery and the challenges faced by women and their families, get **Coupon Cookery** *by Prudence Penny. Published in 1943, the book is filled with patriotic poems, point stretching strategies, advice, condolences, and ration point charts. The recipes are generally unexciting, but remember that the men were gone to war and the women had defense jobs. Many mothers now raised their young on their own and grew and canned their family's food in their spare time. Who had the time or energy to cook...even if they could get ingredients?*

6 large potatoes	Salt and pepper to taste
2 Tbs. butter	6 Tbs. grated cheese
½ cup milk	Paprika
1 egg yolk, slightly beaten	

Pare, cook, and mash potatoes until smooth. Add butter, salt, pepper, hot milk, and egg. Beat until light. Make into cones about three inches high or shape with pastry tube on greased baking dish. In the top of each potato cone, make a deep indentation. Mix grated cheese with a little paprika and fill each cone. Bake in hot oven until cheese melts and browns slightly. Serves 6

1940's

EFFIE'S SQUASH RELISH

Effie Price is my good friend who was born and raised in the hand-hewn log cabin we bought a few years ago in the North Carolina mountains. With many years of practice in the kitchen, she's as good a country cook as you'll ever meet. Effie was a member of her local home demonstration club for 30 years. These clubs started up during WWII to assist homemakers in preserving their Victory Garden produce safely.

12 cups grated or chopped squash (she uses yellow)
4 cups chopped onions
4 bell peppers, chopped
¾ cup hot banana or jalapeno peppers, chopped
5 Tbs. plain salt

Sprinkle salt over vegetables and refrigerate overnight. In the morning, rinse and drain. Bring to boil 2/3 cup vinegar, 4½ cups sugar, 1½ tsp. celery seed, 1 tsp. tumeric, 1 Tbs. dry mustard, and ½ tsp. black pepper. Add vegetables and bring to a boil. Simmer 20 minutes. Can or refrigerate.

How to
S-T-R-E-T-C-H
a Point

*There are problems of arithmetic
And problems of good sense
There are problems of a victory
And problems of defense
But of all life's major problems
And it still may cause dismay
Is how to stretch a ration point
And eat three meals a day!*

1940's

AUNT JENNY

The Spry Way is My Way

Aunt Jenny, 1942

"Cooking the Spry way eliminates waste and failures. And pure, bland Spry lets you get all the rich, delicious flavor from your ingredients...doesn't cover up as ordinary shortenings may."

And nobody cooks better the Spry way than Aunt Jenny! Spry shortening sponsored the popular radio show, "Aunt Jenny's Real Life Stories" which aired on CBS from 1937 to 1956. Aunt Jenny told a complete story in fifteen minute segments, Monday through Friday of each week. My favorite of all the old advertising cooking personalities, the Aunt Jenny character portrays a southern, spicy, wise, down-home woman whose Spry cookbooks scream World War II era nostalgia. Some of the recipes are good, too, especially if you substitute butter for the solid shortening. The booklets are easy to find. They'll entertain you, I promise.

Aunt Jenny, 1949

Aunt Jenny gets a more well-behaved, professional look for the 1950's.

"START ENJOYING FRIED FOODS TODAY!"

1940's

SPRY IS **ALWAYS** SOFT AN' EASY TO CREAM.. WHY, YOU'LL SAY IT'S SO WONDERFULLY CREAMY THAT YOUR CAKE'S MIXED AS IF BY MAGIC. AN' IT COMES OUT OF THE OVEN AS LIGHT AS A FEATHER

CHOCOLATE ORANGE CRUNCHIES

1 cup Spry (shortening)	1 cup brown sugar, packed
1¼ tsp. salt	1 egg
1 Tbs. orange rind	2 cups flour
2 Tbs. orange juice	¼ tsp. baking soda
½ cup nuts, chopped	

8-ounce bar semisweet chocolate chopped

Blend Spry, salt, rind, and juice. Add sugar gradually and cream well. Add egg and beat. Sift flour with soda and add to creamed mixture. Add nuts and chocolate, and blend. Drop from spoon on baking sheets rubbed with Spry pan-coat. Bake in a 375° oven 12 minutes until browned. Makes 3 dozen.

Author's Note: This much Spry will clog up something you surely need. I recommend cutting the shortening to ¾ cup (butter is fine, really) and changing the sugar to ½ cup white, ½ cup brown.

1940's

CHOCOLATE APRICOT COOKIES

From Gettleman Brewing Company's 1944 **100 No-Butter Cookie Recipes** *advertising cookbooklet. Don't get excited. No-butter means white shortening; butter being particularly difficult to get during the war. Being a butter-snob, I was surprised to find these cookies excellent in flavor and chewiness, and not nearly as good when made with butter. Chocolate chips aren't original to the recipe, but they add an extra chocolate zing.*

½ cup shortening   1 tsp. baking powder
1 cup white sugar   ½ tsp. salt
1 egg   1½ cups flour
1 square baking chocolate 1/3 cup milk
½ to 1 cup diced, dried apricots 1 tsp. vanilla
½ cup chocolate chips, melted

Cream shortening and sugar. Add egg and blend. Melt baking chocolate and add to creamed mixture along with the milk and vanilla. Beat in baking powder, salt, then flour. Melt chocolate chips and stir into batter along with the apricots. Drop by spoonfuls onto parchment paper and bake at 350° about 12 minutes or until done. Makes about 3 dozen little cookies.

1940's

SPICY APPLE PIE

6 large tart apples, sliced
   thin
1 cup sugar (I'd use ½ cup)
1 tsp. cinnamon
½ tsp. nutmeg
Pinch salt
1 tsp. lemon juice
1 Tbs. butter

Line a 9-inch pie pan with pastry. Fill pie shell with sliced apples. Mix sugar, spices, salt, and lemon juice and sprinkle over apples. Dot with butter. Moisten edge of pie crust with water and fit top crust over apples, sealing the edge of the pie. Bake in a hot (400°) oven 40-45 minutes until apples bubble and crust is nicely browned.

Aunt Jenny looks like she's up to something. I'm a little nervous about that big knife.

SPRY FLAKY PIE CRUST

2½ cup flour	¾ cup Spry (shortening)
1 tsp. salt	5 Tbs. cold water

Cut salt and shortening into flour until particles are the size of navy beans. Add just enough water to moisten. Divide dough into two balls, handling as little as possible. Find a mama who makes good pies to show you the art of rolling and crimping a pie crust.

WEIRD LITTLE SANDWICHES

"Canape sandwiches are served usually in the drawing room or living room with cocktails, although they are sometimes placed on the individual service plates at the table. In either case, they are also passed at the table by the maid or butler at the beginning of the meal."
The Heinz Salad Book, 1940's

TONGUE SANDWICH
"Grind cold boiled tongue, using a coarse cutter, and moisten with mayonnaise. Spread on thin slices of white bread."

GREEN PEPPER SANDWICHES
"Three green peppers, three hard boiled eggs, chopped fine. Mix with a small cup of mayonnaise. Put between slices of buttered bread."

PIMENTO BUTTER SANDWICH
"Cream ¼ cup butter and add 2 canned pimentos which have been forced through a puree strainer. When thoroughly blended, season with ¼ tsp. salt."

RAW CARROT SANDWICH
"Peel and grate raw carrots, mix with salt, red pepper, and mayonnaise—enough to make quite soft. Spread thick on bread."

Loyal Workers Cookbook, 1929

WEIRD LITTLE SANDWICHES

SPARTON SANDWICH CAKES

Each lucky guest gets one of these. "Cut bread in 2½ inch squares. Make sandwiches four decks high and use a different filling in between each of the two slices of bread (you'll have three layers of filling). Frost the entire sandwich with colored whipped cream cheese."

Note: If you want to make the cake in this picture, make yourself some pink bread and frost with white cream cheese.

Matilda's Proven Sparton Refrigerator Recipes, 1930's

This is a tomato, lettuce, ham, banana, and gherkin sandwich. If the children don't like that, perhaps they'll go for this facewich.

GRILLED "P-B-C" SANDWICH, 1940's

"Use three slices of bacon for each sandwich. Toast slices of bread on one side only. Spread untoasted side with peanut butter, then with chili sauce. Top with slices of bacon,

the edges of which have been notched with a knife to prevent curling. Broil slowly until the bacon is slightly browned and crisp. Serve immediately with slices of gherkins."

FOODS THAT WIGGLE

MAKE MY STOMACH JIGGLE

My mother loves opaque, wiggly foods. Things like tapioca pudding (which, as kids, my sisters and I called eyeball pudding), custards, and souffles are her favorites. I personally would rather wash all the windows in the house than eat one spoonful of tapioca pudding. However, I realize that you might like wobbly, fluffy foods. So I'm including them in this chapter along with some other transparent wiggly foods that were popular in the early 20th century that will amaze your innards.

MOM'S LEMON MERINGUE PIE

This is my mother's idea of a great birthday cake. It was her mother's recipe. If you don't have a large lemon, use two smaller ones.

1 cup sugar	3 egg yolks (save the whites)
3 Tbs. flour	1 cup water
1 large lemon, juice & rind	1 Tbs. butter

Combine flour and sugar. Beat egg yolks and add to flour and sugar mixture along with remaining ingredients. Cook on medium heat stirring constantly, until it starts to simmer. Then turn heat to low and cook until thickened. Cool and pour into cooked and cooled pie shell.

Meringue
Beat 3 egg whites, ¼ tsp. cream of tartar and dash of salt until stiff, but not dry. Add 6 Tbs. sugar gradually while beating until it stands in stiff peaks. Cover pie well, including edges. Bake at 450° about 5 minutes until lightly browned.

Knox Gelatin (1915)
"The pies and hot puddings of our grandmother's days have waned in popularity, and in their places are to be found cold and frozen desserts."

FOODS THAT WIGGLE

DO YOU HAVE FEAR OF PIES?

J ust when I thought I'd seen the best of the advertising cookbooks, I found this one from 1938: **Aunt Chick's Pies**. It seems that Mrs. Samuel Pendleton McBirney (Aunt Chick), food editor for the *Tulsa Daily World*, had become frustrated with the pies she was turning out. You know how terrible a soggy crust can be. In fact, her research indicated that "nine out of ten women were afraid of pies." So she invented the *Crispy Crust Pie Pan* which was a tin pan with a wire mesh bottom to "eliminate the scare from them forever."

Aunt Chick was a hoot, and the book is quite funny, but she was serious about her pies. And they are good ones. I'm including a couple Chiffon pie recipes from her book because they were popular in the 1930's and they fit into the foamy, opaque wiggly food category.

CHERRY CHIFFON PIE

"Scald together ½ cup sugar, 1 Tbs. gelatine, 1 cup canned cherry juice, 1½ cups cherries, 1 Tbs. lemon juice, ¼ tsp. salt. Cool. When beginning to set, fold in ½ cup heavy cream, whipped stiff. Pour cooled mixture into a baked pie shell."

Mrs. Samuel Pendleton McBirney

CHOCOLATE CHIFFON PIE

"Combine, beat with Dover egg-beater until chocolate is blended and then cook to custard, ½ cup sugar, 1 Tbs. gelatine, ½ tsp. salt, 2 squares baking chocolate, ¾ cup milk, 3 yolks. Cool. As it begins to set, fold in 3 egg whites stiffly beaten with ¼ cup sugar. Pour into baked shell. Top with whipped cream."

Author's Note: Uncooked egg whites can make you sick. It's best to use powdered or substitute whipped cream.

FOODS THAT WIGGLE

W ith the passage of the Pure Food and Drug Act in 1906, there came a renewed interest in wholesome foods and healthier bodies. No longer were plump women and portly men the fashion rage. Housewives were reminded by popular food companies that they had better things to do than slave over the hot stove all day. They should serve their families dainty, light, easy to prepare desserts made with gelatin.

Lime Mallow Sponge

Though gelatin dishes had been around for some time, Jell-O revolutionized the see-through wiggly dessert when it stormed onto the food scene in 1902 in an advertising blitz with its raspberry, strawberry, orange, and lemon flavors. In the early Jell-O days, recipe books encouraged housewives to combine the fruit flavored powders with actual fruit. Slowly but surely, cucumbers, tomatoes, olives, radishes, and the like sneaked their way into the lemon flavored gelatin.

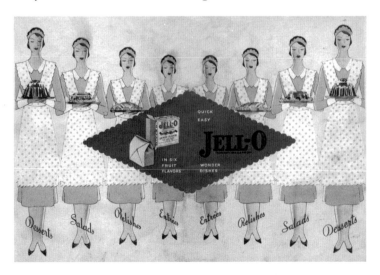

FOODS THAT WIGGLE

_ᴥ_

Things heated up in 1930 when Jell-O unleashed their lime flavor. What started out as an innocent Lime Mallow Sponge (see lovely drawing left) evolved into dishes such as the one below. You should be glad this is not a color photograph. I've included the recipe in its entirety so you can get the full effect of the unusual combination of savory, sour, and sweet flavors.

CABBAGE AND GRAPEFRUIT SALAD, 1945

1 pkg. lime Jell-O
2 cups hot water
1 cup grapefruit sections, free from membranes
1 tablespoon vinegar
2 tablespoons sugar
1 tablespoon horseradish
1 cup finely shredded cabbage
¼ cup stuffed olives

Dissolve Jell-O in hot water. Chill until slightly thickened. Turn about ¼ cup Jell-O into large mold, and in it arrange grapefruit sections. Chill until firm. Then combine the questionable vegetable mixture and add to the thickened Jell-O. Garnish with escarole and radish roses. Serve with mayonnaise. Yummy!

Foods That Wiggle

The Neuroscience of Green Jell-O

Did you know that in 1997 real scientists hooked a bowl of green Jell-O up to an EEG machine? Besides the obvious finding that these science technicians had too much time on their hands, they discovered that the Jell-O waves almost identically matched the brain waves of healthy adult humans.

Sauerkraut Jell-O, 1938

2 cups sauerkraut
Juice ½ lemon
1 pkg. lemon Jell-O
1/8 teaspoon salt
1 cup boiling water
1/8 teaspoon paprika

Dissolve a packet of lemon Jell-O in one cup of boiling water. When cool add sauerkraut, lemon juice, salt and paprika. Fill individual molds or cups. Chill. This recipe will make six individual molds. At serving time, remove from molds. Cut in any desired shapes and use as a garnish for salads or cold meats.

FOODS THAT WIGGLE

CORNED TONGUE IN ASPIC, 1915

I won't go into the details, but the general idea is to cover a cooked, cooled, corned tongue with layers of aspic, boiled eggs, pistachio nuts, and truffles. You then decorate the tasty morsel with green sauterne jelly to represent moss and curled celery to represent feathers. Voila! A gleaming, nesting avian tongue.

Dainty Desserts, Knox Gelatin, 1915

WHAT'S FOUND ONLY IN JELL-O?

When my mother-in-law, Lori Erbsen, was a child (in the 1920's), Jell-O desserts were all the rage at birthday parties. She says, "I wasn't about to eat that shaky looking thing," and all the kids knew it. Competition was fierce for the seats next to Lori at the party table as the children vied for her portion of Jell-O.

Lori Erbsen in 1935

FOODS THAT WIGGLE

TUNA FISH SALAD, 1915

Won't your friends be surprised when you bring these jellied tuna Martians to the potluck luncheon?

MOCHA CHARLOTTE, JELL-O 1922

Unfortunately, chocolate flavored Jell-O was discontinued in 1926, but you can make your own by adding cocoa powder and sugar to unflavored gelatin. Or you can make chocolate pudding and add a spoonful of instant coffee to the milk and top it with the suggestions below.

"Dissolve one package chocolate Jell-O in 1¾ cups moderate strength coffee which has been strained through a fine cloth and heated to a boiling point. Add the Jell-O slowly, stirring meanwhile, and add a pinch of salt. When cold and beginning to thicken, add one teaspoonful vanilla and ½ cup heavy whipped cream. Mold in individual molds. Serve with whipped cream or plain cream slightly sweetened, or custard dressing. Nutmeats and diced marshmallows may be added to it or used as a garnish."

No Way!
~

Children's Ice Cream Flavors, 1947

Watercress Sherbet
Spinach Ice Cream
Carrot Ice Cream

340 Recipes for the New Waring Blender

Brains & Eggs

"Cut beef brains into small pieces and simmer. Add to onions and parsley that have been cooked in butter. Then add eggs and cook until set. Serve on toast."

Penny Tip: Brains may be crumbled and fried like sweetbreads.

    Good, too!   Coupon Cookery, 1942

Author's Note: DON'T EAT BRAINS! You could contract a fatal illness from eating them!

Orange Whey

Heat one pint sweet milk and the juice of two oranges slowly until curds are formed; strain and cool before drinking.

             Quick Cooking, 1900

To the Modern Housewife, 1927

In bread baking as in baseball, there is nothing
Like a good batter in the hour of knead.

We may live without poetry, music and art
We may live without conscience and live without heart
We may live without friends, we may live without books,
But civilized man cannot live without cooks.

HEALTH & REMEDIES

SUMMER COMPLAINT

Here is an actual page from **Dr. Caldwell's Home Cook Book**, published shortly after 1906. This trusted purveyor of Dr. Caldwell's Syrup Pepsin asks that "the housewives of America accept this book with his compliments so that they may find something among the recipes to add to the pleasure of the family dinner."

Notice the close proximity of the recipes to the graphic descriptions of various stomach miseries cured by Syrup Pepsin. This is not my idea of dining pleasure. I can no longer eat Green Tomato Mince Meat for thinking about various griping pains of unmentionable body parts. Can you?

HEALTH & REMEDIES

Dr. Caldwell's Syrup Pepsin is one of the finest medicines I have ever used.—C. L. Carty, East Radford, Pa.

Summer Complaint

As the name summer complaint indicates, this disease is peculiar to the warm season. It may be caused by impure water, unripe fruit or over-ripe fruit and vegetables. There are griping pains in the stomach, vomiting and purging, and very loose bowels. The stools are griping and painful, free and very watery, though they occur with unnatural frequency. No better or simpler remedy for this condition can be found than Dr. Caldwell's Syrup Pepsin. You should take it at the first sign of summer complaint, as the frequency of the stools is very weakening, and unless checked some serious trouble is liable to result.

Bad Breath

Bad breath may be caused by decayed teeth or food lodged in the mouth and decomposing, but as a general rule some digestive trouble is the cause of it, and that being so the surest remedy to cure it is Dr. Caldwell's Syrup Pepsin.

Sick Headache

There are various forms of headache and vertigo, or, as it is often called, dizziness. The nervous, sick headache is nine

RECIPES---Continued

Green Tomato Mince Meat

I pk. green tomatoes, 1 lb. sugar, 1 lb. currants, 1 tbsp. cloves, 2 tsp. nutmeg, 1 cup suet, 1 cup vinegar, 5 lbs. "C" sugar, 1 lb. raisins, 2 tbsp. ground cinnamon, 1 tbsp. salt, 1 tsp. ginger, 1 cup boiled cider. Chop tomatoes and drain. Put in cold water and bring to a scald and drain; again cover with cold water, bring to a scald and drain. Then take tomatoes, raisins, currants, suet, sugar and salt and cook 1 hour. Add cider, vinegar and spices. Cook down as thick as you like. Put in jars and seal.

What to Serve With Meats

Roast Beef—Grated Horseradish.
Roast Mutton—Currant jelly.
Boiled Mutton—Caper Sauce.
Roast Pork—Apple sauce.
Roast Lamb—Mint sauce.
Venison or Wild Duck—Black Currant jelly.
Roast Goose—Apple sauce.
Roast Turkey—Oyster sauce.
Roast Chicken—Bread sauce.
Compote of Pigeon—Mushroom sauce.
Broiled Fresh Mackerel—Sauce of stewed gooseberries.
Broiled Bluefish—White cream sauce.
Broiled Shad—Rice.
Fresh Salmon—Green peas with cream sauce.

Vegetables

Potatoes Au Gratin

Make 1 cup white sauce; cut 1 pt. cold boiled potatoes in

When a Laxative is needed use Dr. Caldwell's Syrup Pepsin.

HEALTH & REMEDIES

ARE YOU SLUGGISH OF THOUGHT?

"Many young girls and older women suffer from headache, dizziness, sluggishness of thought, and disposition to sleep, with pains in the back and lower limbs and general nervousness and irritability. All of these symptoms are an indication of diseased kidneys. Take Parker's Sure Kidney Pills."

Sloan's Cook Book, 1905

A RACE OF BETTER WIVES AND MOTHERS

"With proper attention to diet and exercise, a race of better wives and mothers is assured. If however, ailments develop, Lydia Pinkham's Vegetable Compound may be depended on to overcome them."

How Phyllis Grew Thin, 1920's

HUMORS AREN'T FUNNY

"Humors and eruptions are among the most common indications and results of poor blood. They are very unpleasant and disfiguring. Eat plain, easily digested food and take Lydia E. Pinkham's Blood Medicine one-half hour before meals."

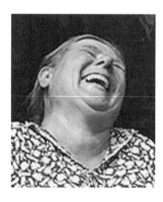

MRS. WHITNEY'S DYSPEPTIC PUDDING, 1901

"One pint graham flour. A pinch of salt. One quart applesauce, thinned with boiling water. Boil together ten minutes. Serve with warm cream or milk and sugar."

HEALTH & REMEDIES

T he Spanish Flu pandemic of 1918-19 was a global disaster, killing well over 20 million people worldwide. The virus first surfaced in Fort Riley, Kansas, in March of 1918, though some speculate it originated in China. The flu traveled to Europe with soldiers as Americans engaged in WWI creating far more casualties than the war itself. Children could be heard jumping rope to rhymes such as this one:

I had a little bird,
Its name was Enza
I opened the window
And in-flew-Enza.

Legislators were bombarded by requests from citizens for laws that forbid sneezing and coughing in public. Public gatherings were banned in Washington, D.C., and citizens throughout the country were required to wear face masks in public, which were useless because viruses are so small. Feeling powerless against this plague, people concocted all manner of remedies to prevent loved ones from contracting the flu. Children were bathed in onions. Elixirs of turpentine and herbs were dropped onto sugar cubes. The flu left America as quickly as it arrived and even though most every family was touched by it, the disease was quickly forgotten.

Are You a Weary Mother?

O weary mothers rolling dough,
Don't you wish that food would grow.
How happy all the world would be,
With a cookie bush
*   and a doughnut tree.*

HOUSEHOLD HINTS

WASHING DELICATES, 1905

Now hands need *never* touch mop water

"Colored silks should be washed in gasoline or naptha, out of doors and rinsed well in clean gasoline."

"If you have some gasoline left over from cleaning clothes; pour down the sink and follow with hot water. Grease deposits will be cut loose."

A MIRACLE COMES TO THE KITCHEN, 1941

"You've dreamed of it! You've hoped for it! And maybe you thought the day would never come! But here it is, another miracle for today's busy homemaker. Never again need you spend precious time washing and trimming spinach or shelling lima beans. For now these grand vegetables come right to you, farm-fresh and scrupulously clean, ready to cook. What is this miracle? It's Birds Eye Quick Frozen Foods!"

"Glamorous is a word that is overworked but here's one place where it really belongs. Try luscious Birds Eye Peaches held in a shining mold of Orange Jell-O."

HOUSEHOLD HINTS

DON'TS FOR THE HOSTESS, 1927

- *Never fry food. Broil, boil or bake meats, fish, or vegetables.*
- *Use as little salt as possible.*
- *Use mineral oil where salad oil is required for vegetable salad.*
- *Never make a gelatin dessert stiff.*
- *Never serve any cheese except Roquefort or Cottage Cheese.*

THAT UNCERTAIN BOILED ICING, 1905

"Every housewife knows the perfect boiled icing is the most difficult thing to make. Try this. In making chocolate boiled icing, if it gets too hard, don't boil the second time, just add a little cream gradually and it will stir to proper smoothness. This method will solve the icing problem."

Leave your oven door open a few minutes to let steam out and let dry. It will not rust so easily.

A child should not be weaned in the hot months.

At ten months, the child can be fed some gruels.

Sloan's Cook Book and Advice to Housekeepers, 1905

BIBLIOGRAPHY

1900-1919

65 Delicious Dishes Made with Bread, Fleischmann Co., 1919
A Few Cooking Suggestions, Crisco, 1910's
Choice Recipes, Walter Baker & Co., 1916
Dainty Desserts for Dainty People, Knox Gelatin 1915
Dr. Caldwell's Guide to Health Home Cook Book, 1906
Good Things to Eat Made with Bread, The Fleischmann Co., 1914
Larkin Housewives Cookbook, 1915
Quick Cooking, A Book of Culinary Heresies, 1900
Royal Baker and Pastry Cook, 1911
Snowdrift Secrets, Sara Tyson Rorer, 1913
Sunkist Recipes, 1916
Welch Ways, Welch Grape Juice Company, 1915

1920s

100 Delights, Dromedary Food Products, 1922
Aunt Sammy's Radio Recipes, USDA, 1927
Daughters of Isabella Cookbook, Hays, Kansas, 1927
Delicious Quick Desserts, The Junket Folks, 1929
Electric Refrigerator Recipes, General Electric, 1927
From the Heart of the Wheat, Mueller Company, 1924
Good Things to Eat, Wesson Oil and Snowdrift, 1926
Jell-O, America's Most Famous Dessert at Home Everywhere, 1922
Lutes, Della Thompson, The Presto Book of Menus & Recipes, 1929
Proven Recipes, Corn Products Refining Company, 1920s
New Calendar of Salads, Elizabeth O. Hiller, 1920s
New Home Cook Book, Oven Cooking for Wood, Gas, Electricity 1925
Reliable Recipes, Calumet, 1920
Swans Down Cake Manual, 1928
The Art of Making Bread, Northwestern Yeast Company, 1920s

OTHER

Duke Library, Emergence of Advertising in America 1850-1920,
Nicole Di Bona Peterson Collection of Early Advertising Cookbooks.
This wonderful site includes 82 digitized cookbooks from 1878-1929.
http://scriptorium.lib.duke.edu/eaa

BIBLIOGRAPHY

1930s

57 Unusual Ways to Serve Spaghetti, 1933
88 Mealtime Surprises Made with Bond Bread, 1931
Aunt Chick's Pies, 1938
Bananas in Attractive New Dishes for the Up-to-Date Housewife, 1930s
Brer Rabbit's Modern Recipes for the Modern Hostess, 1930s
Good Things to Eat, Arm & Hammer Baking Soda, 1933
Lutes, Della, The Country Kitchen, 1937
Matilda's Proven Sparton Recipes, Sparton Refrigerators, 1930s
Modern Modes in Meat Cookery, National Livestock Board, 1934
New Delights from the Kitchen, Kelvinator, 1930s
Presto Recipe Book, Presto Cake Flour, 1937
Quality Cook Book, Roberts & Mander Gas Stove Company, 1930s
Sauerkraut as a Health Food, National Kraut Pakers Assoc. 1930s
Tested and Proven Recipes, Mueller's, 1933
The Plus Food for Minus Meals, Kelloggs All-Bran Cereal, 1930s
Tummy Tingles, The Wheat Flour Institute, 1937

1940s

100 No-Butter Cookie Recipes, Gettelman Brewing Co., 1944
101 Ways to Prepare Macaroni, La Rosa Macaroni Products, 1942
340 Recipes for the New Waring Blendor, 1947
Birds Eye Cook Book, 1941
Electric Cooking with Your Hotpoint Automatic Range, 1940s
Good Cooking Made Easy, Spry, 1942
Kerr, Home Canning Book, Wartime Edition, 1940s
Malone, Dorothy, How Mama Could Cook!, 1946
Metropolitan Cook Book, 1942
Penny, Prudence, Coupon Cookery, 1943
Royal Cookbook (Wartime Version), 1942
Spry, Aunt Jenny's Favorite Recipes, 1940s
Spry, Enjoy Good Eating Every Day, 1949
Spry, Good Cooking Made Easy, 1942
Spry, What Shall I Cook Today?, 1940s
The Way to a Man's Heart, Nashville Gas Company, 1949
Wartime-Ration Recipes for Delicious Meals, Pet Milk Company, 1943

FINDING VINTAGE COOKBOOKS

Bibliofind, a division of Amazon Books
www.bibliofind.com
On-line search site for new, used, out-of-print, and rare books.

Bookfinder
www.bookfinder.com
On-line search site for new, used, out-of-print, and rare books.

Ebay, on-line auctions
www.ebay.com
The best source for old advertising cookbooks. Before I bid on an Ebay item, I check availability at the above sites to see what my bidding limit should be. Although, I've found some wonderful deals, you can easily pay more at auction than through a used book store.

Acanthus Books
www.acanthus-books.com (847) 726-9811
830 W. Main St. #150, Lake Zurich, IL, 60047
Cookbook reprints, fascimilies, culinary history books

Food Heritage Press
www.foodbooks.com (978) 356-8306
Catalog $1.00, send to:
Food Heritage Press, P.O. Box 163 Ipswich, MA, 01938-0163
New, out-of-print, reprints of cookbooks, and culinary history books.

Antique malls and stores
Look for booths selling cooking items, they often sell cookbooks, too.

Auctions
This is where you find the best handwritten cookbooks and recipe card files. You may have to buy boxes of books you don't want to get what you do want. Try selling the extra books to your local used book store.

Yard Sales, especially church fundraising yard sales
Older members of the congregation often donate their cookbooks.

CREDITS

A house should have a cookie jar for when it's half past three,
And children hurry home from school as hungry as can be,
There's nothing quite so splendid in filling children up,
As spicy, fluffy ginger cakes and sweet milk in a cup.

A house should have a mother waiting with a hug,
No matter what a boy brings home—a puppy or a bug.
For children only loiter when the bell rings to dismiss,
If no one's home to greet them with a cookie and a kiss.

THANKS!

Thanks to Steve Millard, for cover design and to Nancy Swell, Lori Erbsen, and Effie Price for stories and recipes. Proof readers included McLean Bissell, Dave Currier, Lori Erbsen, Bonnie Neustein, Janet Swell, Nancy Swell, Beverly Teeman, and Jennifer Thomas. Thanks to Leon Swell and Wes Erbsen for all-too-frequent emergency computer support, and to Sara Webb whose line I stole. The tireless taste testers included Annie, Wes, Rita, and Wayne Erbsen, McLean Bissell, Dave Currier, and Ethan Millard (our four-year-old neighbor who really likes the Chocolate Risin' Cake). And finally, thanks to Wayne, my ever-patient publisher and partner in life who hopes that one day I will make him some wiggly Tapioca Pudding!

NATIVE GROUND MUSIC

BOOKS OF SONGS & LORE

Backpocket Bluegrass Songbook
Backpocket Old-Time Songbook
Cowboy Songs, Jokes & Lore
Crawdads & Creasy Greens
Front Porch Songs, Jokes & Stories
Log Cabin Pioneers
Old-Time Gospel Songbook
Outlaw Ballads, Legends, & Lore
The Outhouse Papers
Railroad Fever
Rousing Songs of the Civil War

INSTRUCTION BOOKS

5-String Banjo for the
    Complete Ignoramus!
Starting Bluegrass Banjo
    From Scratch
Bluegrass Banjo Simplified!!
Painless Mandolin Melodies
Southern Mountain Banjo
Southern Mountain Fiddle
Southern Mountain Guitar
Southern Mountain Mandolin
Southern Mountain Dulcimer

RECORDINGS

Authentic Outlaw Ballads
Ballads & Songs of the Civil War
Cold Frosty Morning
Cowboy Songs of the Wild Frontier
Front Porch Favorites
Love Songs of the Civil War
The Home Front
Log Cabin Songs

Old-Time Gospel Favorites
Raccoon and a Possum
Railroadin' Classics
Railroad Fever
Singing Rails
Songs of the Santa Fe Trail
Southern Mountain Classics
Southern Soldier Boy

Other great Native Ground cookbooks by Barbara Swell:
Take Two & Butter 'Em While They're Hot!,
Log Cabin Cooking, Children at the Hearth,
Secrets of the Great Old-Timey Cooks

Write or call for a FREE Catalog:
Native Ground Music
109 Bell Road
Asheville, NC 28805
(800) 752-2656
Web Site: www.nativeground.com
Email: banjo@nativeground.com